ILLUMINATION
By
Annamarie
Vickers

ISBN: 978-0-244-43591-2

Hi everyone, so here is book number nine! I know I here you where has the time gone. It's been a whirlwind of a year for me and you'll find that reflected in much of this year's poetry. Thank you once again for all the support my readers give to me, this year has found me placing my books in a physical shop and I couldn't keep writing without the love and support of my rock Ross Davies and of course my loving family. I hope you enjoy my walk into the light, as after all we all need some colour in our lives.

Lots of Love and Best Wishes
Annamarie Vickers

LIVING
IN THE
SHADOWS

TREADING WATER

You built me up you made me strong,
You made me feel like I belong.
Now all I seem to feel is numb,
An annoying splinter in your thumb.

I thought I was your everything,
Love slipped away with no warning,
I wanted you to hold me tight,
But now I'm just too tired to fight.

Keep trying so hard not to break,
A smile is all too easy to fake.
How could our love turn to dust?
Why did you throw away my trust?

Maybe I expected too much,
Used to revel in your touch.
New chapter, different page,
Take a bow, exit centre stage.

HALFHEARTED LOVE

Is a halfhearted love better, than no love at all?
It's hard to walk tall when you feel so small.
A life of memories in a carrier bag,
I had to surrender and wave the white flag.

Why wasn't I happy? I didn't belong,
How can something so right become so wrong.
I loved you with every beat of my heart,
Now an ocean of hurt swept us miles apart.

So many things that we left unsaid,
Tarnished our dreams and left them for dead.
Though by my side I felt completely alone,
We never had the chance to make a house a home.

I know that I had to say goodbye,
Still I'm waiting for these tears to dry.
A halfhearted love is no love at all,
To rise again you must choose to fall.

NOVEMBER RAIN

My cheek against the window pane,
I wonder do you think of me?
In every drop of November rain,
Is my smile the vision that you see.

A symphony of hopes and dreams,
Sent out into the atmosphere,
Captured by the Autumn leaves,
But all too soon they disappear.

I picture you in the blazing light,
Am I safely held within your heart?
Was there ever a chance I'd win this fight?
Maybe we're meant to be apart.

Illuminations on the horizon,
A wondrous sight that we both see,
But I'm destined to wait here in the dark,
Wondering if you think of me.

CAGED

You snatched away my freedom,
I made just one mistake,
You could have given me shelter,
But you wished to see me break.

Need to taste a little danger,
Release all inhibitions,
Give me the chance to make,
All of the wrong decisions.

No longer a little girl,
The world has left her mark,
I'm stepping away from sunshine,
Embracing a little dark.

Breaking out of this cage,
Focusing on my rebirth,
I ain't going down quietly,
Now I know just what I'm worth.

<u>APOCALYPSE</u>

Lock your doors and shut the windows tight,
Good and evil wage a war tonight,
Who will win this ultimate battle?
Pure fear will cause your bones to rattle.

Where shadows meet the sapphire lake,
The spirits will find their souls to take,
A candle's flame keeps ghosts at bay,
We all have sins they wish us to pay.

Who finally gets to decide our fate?
All depends on which side you wish to take.
The wheel of life in eternal freeze,
A continuous cycle made to tease.

So on the night when this war is fought,
Take the time to give this idea a thought,
If evil was able to take a stand,
We'd forfeit our passage to the promised land.

THE DOTTED LINE

Thought we could weather any storm,
Instead left broken and forlorn.
Nothing more I can express,
You took the best, exiled the rest.

Tired of crying hopeless tears,
For all those wasted loveless years,
We had our heaven long ago,
Hard to hear 'I told you so!'

Maybe you weren't right for me,
Guess I refused to really see,
How twisted our dreams had become,
When I was certain you were the one.

A pile of papers seals our fate,
Try not to let friendship turn to hate,
I'll tell them all 'I'm doing fine'
It's just a signature on a dotted line.

<u>EMBRACE</u>

How can't you see her pain?
In the tracks of her tears are scars naked to the
eye. She's screaming deep inside, but nobody
hears her cry. Can't break out of the enemy's cage,
no matter how hard she tries. Addicted to their
poisonous barb another pure heart dies.

Surely you feel her hurt?
Liquid fire branding with each hurtful word. A
lost soul willing to do anything, to let her voice be
heard.

Can't you see the anguish in her eyes?
She just wants off of this dangerous ride. It's
getting too hard for her to hide. She tries to put on
an epic show. After all it's what she does you
know? But once the foundations move the wall, it
must come tumbling, she lives for the fall. So easy
to just keep looking down, her smile is the face of
a jaded clown. No longer willing to prolong the
fight, she'll accept her fate and embrace the night.

HANDS ARE TIED

Destructive as an earth quake,
Each time I see your heart break,
The smile you give is so fake,
I don't know what to do.

Hard to see you die inside,
God must know how hard you've tried,
Still I see your hands are tied,
I still have faith in you.

Don't concentrate on what went wrong,
I know you feel you don't belong,
Just hold my hand, I'll make you strong,
My love will see you through.

I'll take away your darkest fear,
Make the anxiety disappear,
Whatever happens I will be here,
My love for you is true.

FAITHLESS

Do you think it's fair to take away a life?
To mentally destroy, then twist the knife?
What power have you to make those decisions?
To simply eliminate dreams and ambitions.

It's hard to believe someone so special,
Can be the cause of such hurt and pain,
With a snap of your fingers...poof and gone,
You set up the pawns just to knock them down
again.

Maybe you think it's all a huge game,
From when we're born we should accept our fate,
But we sure as hell didn't sign up for this,
We decline to play, now it's way too late.

So much for faith, where has it got us?
We give our all just for you to snatch it away,
Walking on eggshells, so much for worship,
Guess we're simply irreplaceable at the end of the
day.

I'm tired...of...words, anger burns inside,
It feels like your love for us is a smokescreen and
lies,
You slammed the door, shut out all the light,
We're backed in a corner but we're ready to fight.

HUNTED

Silently they bide their time,
This is not a nursery rhyme,
They're here to snatch away your soul,
From tonight you won't be whole.

Hard to distinguish, just where the cards lay,
Whom is the hunter and whom is the prey.
The metallic stench of human blood,
Calls to the pack huddled deep in the wood.

All ..they ...need.. to do is wait,
For some innocent child to take the bait,
Once they step off the winding path,
They will feel the Soul Reapers wrath.

So if you go down to the park today,
Remember the message I portray,
If you glimpse a shadow don't look back,
When the moon is full they will attack.

SHOT TILL YOU DROP!

With fear in his eyes he weighed up the cost,
The remnants of another awesome night lost,
How did he get here? Back home to his bed?
Tongue like sandpaper and a banging head.

It was your usual average house party,
With pounding music, boyish hilarity,
The heckling and jeering wouldn't stop,
Till he gave in and swallowed a drop.

One... two... three and four,
A pile of glasses littered the floor,
After a few hours stumble to the car,
Not like he had to travel too far.

The beauty needs a lift back to her place,
Perhaps you failed to see my ghostly face.
You swerved to avoid that old oak tree,
That sudden bump in the road was...me.

WALK IN THE LIGHT

FAIRYTALE ENDING

New chapter, chance to start again,
No one knows how this story will end.
A little intrigue sets the pages alight,
Wrapped in love to bind the words tight.

A sprinkling of magic dusts the cover,
You never know what you may discover,
A beacon of truth illuminates the dark,
Hard not to let doubt leave its tainted mark.

Each line is touched by a hint of mystery,
Will the ending just be a repeat of history?
I guess the finale comes down to fate,
Try to keep control but we cannot dictate.

Every fairytale has to have a beginning,
A time to believe and a day of reckoning,
No one knows how the story will end,
I'll write a new chapter, start over again.

STUMBLING

Hard to make the first stumble,
Too easy to anticipate the fall,
Trying to stay independent,
Still learning it's ok to crawl.

Maybe there'll be teething problems,
My surroundings are unfamiliar,
But the darkness begins to fade,
Situations aren't so linear.

Light my life with wondrous colour,
Paint me a picture of harmony,
Chase away the rumbling thunder,
Share your dreams with only me.

Won't you join me on this journey,
Where our hearts beat out of time,
Where every breath is a miracle,
When our hands are intertwined.

ROAD TO DESTINY

Promise you'll be there if I fall,
When our backs are pressed against the wall.
I know that you will take my hand,
Whenever I find it hard to stand.

Say you'll be my curtain call,
When the show is over once and for all.
Illuminate my darkest day,
Only your light can lead the way.

Finally learning it's ok to breathe,
Unbreakable bond from the dreams that we weave.
Waiting so long... just to exhale,
Knowing you'll be there if I should fail.

Navigating this road to destiny,
Together we'll face strong adversity.
But with you I will take this leap of faith,
Ours is a love that will not be erased.

PERFECTLY IMPERFECT

Don't promise me forever,
Or take down the twinkling stars,
No fancy bricks and mortar,
Home is here within your arms.

Masters of our own universe,
Makers of blissful dreams,
We'll forge our path to happiness,
Conquering all that lies between.

With your hand held in mine,
I no longer feel alone,
You brought me back to life,
When despair was overthrown.

Don't promise me perfection,
It cannot be achieved,
There's nothing left to strive for,
If loves easily received.

Heartbreak makes us stronger,
Hidden truths can break us down,
But nothing seems to hurt me,
Now I know that your around.

I don't require a fairytale,
No special kind of fuss,
We are perfectly imperfect,
And that's just fine with us.

MOVING DAY

A house full of snapshots,
Stone walls gathering dreams,
A conscious space of memories,
Bursting at the seams.

Raw pain now sealed away,
In a scuffed up cardboard box,
One day we'll share a smile,
Our emotional equinox.

An imprint left on every room,
Of childhood innocence,
A life of hope, love and loss,
And a world of experience.

Memories packed in bubble wrap,
Safely stored within my heart,
Twisting the key just one last time,
Embracing a brand new start.

COMMITMENT

Carefully you placed your hand
Over mine, still intertwined
Make me smile with every touch
Misty eyed, never ask for much
I belong within your arms
Tempted by your boyish charms
More and more you fill my world
Erased the dark for this little girl,
Never thought I could belong
Till you completed my heart song.

QUIET REFLECTION

I can feel the cold against my skin,
Butterfly kisses on the wind,
Watching people as they go,
Street lights reflect off snow.
Favourite past time
for one and all,
Watching the
snowflakes
fall.

CLAIM THE NIGHT

In your eyes the stars shine bright,
Illuminated by hopes light,
A beacon in the darkest night.

When day has given way to night,
Your aura dims that once shone bright,
Stealing away your golden light.

Long to reignite the light,
That chased away the darkest night,
For once again you must shine bright.

Shine bright starlight and claim the night.

PLEASE SIR!

Please sir if I could be so bold?
I need a moment of your time?
A wool coat to keep out the cold?
Possibly even spare a dime.

There is a chance we may have rain,
My box won't last another night.
Please don't worry I'm not in pain,
These shoes have always been this tight.

What I'd give to feel naked flame,
True warmth against my frozen skin,
But every day still ends the same,
My fairytale, yet to begin.

So sir if you could be so kind,
Remember the child you left behind.

HAIRLINE CRACK

Complete devastation, no warning alarm,
All memories now turned to dust,
Picking up the pieces, of a broken heart,
Valuables tarnished, beginning to rust.

A hairline crack tore our world apart,
A whirlwind sent us in a spin,
You sucked out the love and left a void,
Within this chaos, no one can win.

You shook me from the inside out,
Made me the witness of so much pain,
You took away all that I possessed,
Trying to gather my strength once again.

No longer a victim of your selfish power,
Confusion now left in your wake,
But still I survived the raging heart,
Of a 7.9 earthquake.

MOONSTRUCK

You turn your face away from me,
An age of craters for all to see,
The stories you could tell us all,
When darkness falls we hear your call.

Behind the clouds you shy away,
As gradually night turns into day.
I feel your presence, still you're there,
To capture memories that we share.

Your many cycles soothe my soul,
Constellations stand on patrol,
Lighting the way for their queen,
Who touches the Earth with her silvery gleam.

The tides will change at your whim,
When dawn arrives we welcome him,
But until then you must shine bright,
Guide us with your celestial light.

<u>PURE</u>

Constantly asked to hold my tongue,
Never quite feeling I belong,
Isn't it time I had my say?
Only then will I become strong.

I'm ready to embrace the day,
Let all the chips fall where they may,
Let them believe they control me,
Now I'm here and ready to stay.

See when you look what do you see,
A shadow of the former me,
You walked away and left me here,
But I am pure and flying free.

For now I will not shed a tear,
For all that we once held so dear,
I'll take my leave and disappear,
No longer trapped in deepest fear.

A NEW DAWN

On the November day that I was born,
From peace and serenity I was torn,
My soul was already battered and worn,
Please do not sit at my bedside and mourn.
I see you feeling alone and forlorn,
I'll be soaring high with the birds at dawn.

Raise your face to the sun and welcome dawn,
You gave me a gift the day you were born,
Stopped me from feeling alone and forlorn,
Made me whole once again when I was torn.
Please do not stand at my grave side and mourn,
My physical body was tired and worn.

Do not leave your heart strings tattered and worn,
Take time to repair and embrace the dawn,
Now is no longer the right time to mourn,
For every death another life is born.
I can still see that you feel very torn,
Take your place in this world, don't stand forlorn.

You're wasting your days when you feel forlorn,
Do not count the mistakes that you have worn,
Do not let them leave you confused and torn,

But learn from them and begin a new dawn.
Simply allow yourself to be reborn,
Nothing to regret and nothing to mourn.

By all means give yourself some time to mourn,
It's only natural to feel forlorn,
You exceeded my dreams when you were born,
I can still smell the blanket you had worn,
When I held you until the break of dawn.
Mama has it somewhere faded and torn.

From my loving family I was torn,
I wonder now did my ma sit and mourn?
Did she stay by my cradle till break of dawn?
A shell of a woman, pale and forlorn.
Caressing the garment that I had worn,
Innocently on the day I was born.

The day you were born, twas no longer torn,
Though my soul was worn, not time to mourn.
No longer forlorn, you were my new dawn.

LIFE
IN
COLOUR

SPIDERTASTIC

The following may scare you,
Please don't raise the alarm,
His reputation is mighty suspect,
But he'd never wish you harm.

Me and good old Sidney,
Share a bond you just can't break,
He lives in my dusty attic,
In a cottage beside the lake.

The first time that I saw him,
I was ready to run away,
But he showed me his rare talent,
And I knew I had to stay.

He tapped his way across the floor,
Wibbly wobbling to the beat,
Parading in his New Rock boots,
Tied firmly to his feet.

He may look sort of vicious,
And a little round and chunky,
But the dude learnt to express himself,
So he's really kind of funky.

I know you don't believe me,
So turn down all the lights,
You really cannot miss him,
In his thermal neon tights.

Every night at twelve pm,
He puts on such a show,
If you could see him break dance,
You'd think he was a pro.

He has the entire household,
Hopelessly spellbound,
They really can't resist,
The super spidertastic sound.

THE THUNDER ROLLS

When close just isn't close enough,
Water can be thicker than crimson blood.
I feel you deep within my veins,
Playing my heart strings to your refrain.

Ours is a love that mirrors the stars,
Celestial, otherworldly and hotter than Mars.
Still crave your breath against my skin,
My guiltiest pleasure and darkest sin.

You electrify my heart and soul,
When lightning strikes and thunder rolls.
You are the monsoon to end the drought,
Showed me what butterflies are all about.

When close just isn't close enough,
I'd swim the oceans to feel your touch.
Watch the waves crash against the shore,
To be with you forevermore.

SHOCKWAVES

Your sweet kiss on my lips drives me to distraction, Sending shockwaves down my spine, pure magnetic attraction.

When you pull me close, I'm lost in your orbit, spiraling out of control your touch is my catalyst.

You set my heart to overload, a connection deep within my bones. Left with an insatiable hunger, your power over me strong as thunder.

A tidal wave of emotions but I wouldn't change a thing, you tore down my defenses and taught my heart to sing.

CLOUD SURFING

You vowed to me infinity, whispered promises
against the stars.
Our love is a cosmos of colourful galaxies,
burning ferociously hotter than Mars.

Nothing can extinguish this explosion of senses,
your touch like lightning up and down my spine.
I long to be rocked by your venomous thunder,
ours is a love story that traverses time.

Feels like cloud surfing, the journey we're
embracing still I need to be at the centre of this
storm.
Set my blood racing and body shaking, within
your tornado I'm reborn.

Don't handle me gently, you will not break me,
hold me tightly against your heart.
My shooting star, the light to my dark nothing will
tear our souls apart.

CEREAL KILLER

Set the microwave timer,
Let the breakfast war begin,
Big spoons at the ready,
So the victor can tuck in.

Who will take the title?
That's hanging by a thread,
"Each one to their own,"
Says the butter to the bread.

Tony is up and running,
He can't seem to find his feet!
Slippy sliding on the counter top,
But the flakes are just too sweet.

The Krispies are in tandem,
They're heading for the top,
Crashed straight into the Colonel,
Down with a snap...crackle and pop!

Colonel is in the lead now,
But K has trained to win,
She's counted all the calories,
So she'll somersault the bin.

Mr. Bix conceded long ago,
He's simply just too stodgy,
Bran? Well... what can I say?
Frankly he's a little dodgy.

The bowl is looming up ahead,
You can hear the Charmies cheer,
They tried to cheat by using luck,
Yes, Disqualified this year.

So now it's just the crazy crew,
Never... count out... the loops!
They'll dazzle you with wondrous colour,
Whilst they take out the other troops.

I hope that you've enjoyed the race,
I have been your commentator,
Tune in for more shenanigans,
When Smasher takes on The Tator!!!

CATACLYSMIC SPARK

A kaleidoscope of colours,
Can't express my love for you,
But the light that twinkles in your eye,
Luminates the midnight blue.

You make me feel all warm inside,
When you stoke my bonfire heart,
A gentle touch and cheeky grin,
Simply blows my world apart.

I'm spinning like a Catherine Wheel,
Freewheeling in the dark,
Every time you graze my hand,
A cataclysmic spark.

Our love transcends the universe,
An explosion to rock the night,
Black and white cease to exist,
Now I'm bathed in your celestial light.

GLORY DAYS

As I sit patiently by your side, holding your veiny
hand gently in mine.
I wonder if those rusty cogs, are reliving
memories long lost.
Vacantly you look through me, I could be a ghost
as you're not here right now,
I see eyes etched with the laughter lines of a
young girl,
that forged friendships and experienced love. A
woman in the war and a lady in the home,
the foundations built on a simple upbringing and
hand me down clothes.
A heart that has dealt with sacrifice and pain but
continues to beat.
Family meant everything, and hunger made you
stronger.
Today's modern world must be mass confusion,
hope I can pour my strength into you.
Let you see through my eyes all that you miss.
Listening to the Glory Days.

SUPER DATE

Oh gosh! You'd never believe,
What happened just last week,
I went to close my curtains,
And found I couldn't speak.

Right there upon my windowsill,
I witnessed the strangest sight,
The hunkiest man you'd ever seen,
Decided to land mid-flight.

Well I couldn't believe my luck,
Asked him for a bite to eat,
He murmured "Of course maam"
Preceded to sweep me off my feet!

We flew over the rooftops,
It really was such a thrill,
But wish I'd worn a cardigan,
As it's given me quite a chill.

Where to take him for dinner?
I'm afraid he may stand out,
Don't get me wrong he's mighty fine,
Something to write home about.

I'm worried for the crockery,
What with that super strength,
Maybe we should go Greek?
He could smash till his hearts content.

I wonder where the night could lead,
Do you think he'll want fourth base?
A little kissing and smooching,
Or straight back to my place?

Hope I wore the matching underwear,
Much too late to worry now,
He can x-ray me any day,
I'm dating Superman, Wow!

SOFT TOP I THINK NOT!

Ready, set, ignition fired!
Unleaded fuel is now retired,
Supersonic all the way,
London bound hip hip hooray.

Zooming over rolling hills,
Wish I'd took my sickness pills,
Hold on tight just don't look down!
How do you turn this thing around?

Missing my fluffy steering wheel,
Even my brakes that used to squeal,
Too many controls on this complex dash,
Its inevitable...we're going to crash.

See my dream was to own a flying car,
With super technology not a wish too far,
But Chitty Chitty Bang Bang this is not!
My husband thinks I've lost the plot!

He'd have preferred a house on the moon,
There'd be more chance of a raging typhoon,
Now I'm thinking he may have been right,
No breathing space and it corners too tight.

Don't get me started on how to park,
Imagine their faces as we loom out the dark,
Another thought, I'm considerably wetter,
Maybe a hatchback would have been better.

LADY LUCK

Bets please, don't hesitate,
Is it luck or is it fate?
Another role of the dice.
Kiss them once, shake them twice.

Call the cards and watch them fall,
One more Victor standing tall,
A royal flush to take them down,
A silent prayer makes not a sound.

Breaths are held, and fingers crossed,
Sullen faces when all hopes lost,
The chips are wasted sorrow builds,
Nothing left to pay the bills.

So take a spin with lady luck,
If you think your game enough?
The ball will hover where it may,
Will you prosper, will you pay?

NATURE'S GIFTS

I'd like to give thanks to the stars up above,
For erasing the darkness and igniting my
love.

I'd like to give thanks to my heart that beats,
For letting you have more than the back seat.

I'd like to give thanks to the sun in the sky,
For keeping dreams warm, never letting
them die.

But most of all I'd like to thank you,
For being my shelter as one became two.

KNOWLEDGE IS POWER

So close to the goal I can taste victory,
One step away from our liberty,
Freedom is right at the tip of my tongue,
Just one more chance to get it wrong.

Will all this pain have been for nothing?
Doesn't matter now, we fought for something!
Can feel the blood pump through my veins,
Like a child gorging on candy canes.

Adrenaline finds its way to the heart,
To witness great change, there must be a start,
We gave our all to win this race,
Simply cannot accept second place.

Today we forge our destiny,
Carve our names in history,
Welcome a new world to the field,
Knowledge is the power that we wield.

CALL OF THE SEA

In my dreams I hear you calling me,
Down to the shore I go willingly,
Standing on my parapet,
Remembering the day that we first met.

Your spray still lingers on my skin,
That salty smell buried deep within,
I must seem very small to you,
A dot against the midnight blue.

I'm drowning slowly in your depths,
As you command utmost respect,
Gradually we become one,
Floating towards the eternal sun.